NORTH CAPE

The top of Europe

MORTENSEN

FOREWORD

North Cape. Even the name has a touch of drama. Think about it, and you visualize steep rocky walls and churning sea. Forces of nature unfolding freely. Space without limits – ocean, land and sky untouched by history and the work of man.

Dwell upon the name a little longer, and you see some more: Warm summer days with a sun that never sets. Intense colors and tiny idyllic scenes in the great nature. Tens of thousands of sea birds in elegant flight above coast, fjord and inlet.

Thereafter autumn days with hurricanes, when the colors are washed out and everything becomes shades of black, gray and frothing white.

Then follows the polar winter with snow lashing at your face, with a sun that never rises above the horizon – and a moon that shines around the clock. Clear, cold nights when the northern lights throw red, blue, yellow and green flames across the sky.

Finally darkness yields to spring. Once again the intense light flows freely, one more time North Cape emerges as the towering landmark, the point of intersection between East and West, Europe's spearhead toward the Arctic and the North Pole.

All of this you can imagine through your own fantasy. But you have to go there yourself to realize the intense feelings that arise inside a person who arrives at the very edge of the cliff – and the world. Right there, you are surrounded by the eternal, never-changing nature, the almighty elements that make you humble and reflective.

Yet at the same time, North Cape is but a small part of Finnmark county. Larger than all of Denmark, it offers infinitely varied and unique experiences all year around. This book will take you through that land of contrasts and excitement.

North Cape is an excellent spot for observations of midnight sun, northern lights, sparkling moonlight and astronomical phenomena. July 22nd, 1990, was, however, quite special: Against an almost cloudless sky, spellbound tourists at 3 AM could watch a nearly total eclipse of the sun. More than a hundred years must pass before a similar phenomenon will once again be visible from North Cape.

The steel globe has become the very symbol of North Cape – it has even been reproduced on stamps. In good weather, you can climb inside it and have your picture taken. But when arctic storms rush in from the ocean, the one ton globe can rotate so rapidly that all you see is a blurred shadow.

CONTENTS:

◄ *The kind of North Cape sum-*
mer night you will never for-
get: A glowing sun above a
slumbering Arctic Ocean.
The light, colors and dimen-
sions are overwhelming. For
those who share in this expe-
rience, the time stands still...

Simon Flem Devold and Anton Pet-san, one of the seven Children of the Earth, *next to* Bird of Peace, *which Anton created.*

CHILDREN OF THE EARTH – A UNIQUE PROJECT

Not only does the cliff at North Cape constitute the end of a continent – it also marks the beginning of a unique project for the good of destitute children everywhere.

It started in 1988, when author Simon Flem Devold flew around the globe, picked a young child at random from Brazil, Tanzania, Japan, Italy, the US, Thailand and Russia, and brought them to North Cape. Their unceremonious task was to create, in clay, a relief with a self-elected motive. Devold's purpose was to show that children from dissimilar cultures can cooperate, create something and express happiness across all frontiers – as long as they have not been influenced by the prejudices of grown-ups. SAS and Finnmark county supported the project.

The seven *Children of the Earth*, as they were soon called, have long since returned to their home countries. But on the naked cliff facing the Arctic their works of art, now cast in bronze, framed by granite and anchored to the bedrock, remain as thought-provoking mementos.

At these monuments, an annual Children of the Earth Prize is now awarded to refugee children or other children who suffer somewhere in the world. Behind the prize stands the independent Children of the Earth Foundation, working in conjunction with key Norwegian authorities, the UN High Commissioner for Refugees in Geneva, etc. The prize money, a minimum of 100 000 kroner per year, derives from donations to the foundation's fund from individuals and institutions in many countries. The means are channeled unabridged to sound, well-arranged projects that relieve the suffering and create a future for small children who undeservedly have become victims of war and distress.

North Cape is also home of the Children of the Earth Club. Any child may join. Through the club, members can communicate with each other and suggest ideas for helping less fortunate children in the world. For more information, write to:
Children of the Earth Foundation, The North Cape Hall, 9764 Nordkapp, Norway.

Sculptress Eva Rybakken worked closely with the Children of the Earth who created the seven reliefs at North Cape. Later she made the statue Mother and Child, *giving the whole monument its final, harmonious and symbolic form.*

Standing by the globe on North Cape, you are on 71 degrees, 10 minutes and 21 seconds northern latitude. You are as far north as central Greenland, the northern tip of Baffin Land in the Canadian Arctic, Point Barrow in Alaska and the coast of Siberia. And you can drive here in your own car!

COLORFUL HISTORY

North Cape got its present name in 1553, when the English captain Richard Chancellor sailed around Finnmark, looking for a northern sea route to Asia. A storm forced him off course and close by a magnificent cliff known as Knyskanes among the local people. Chancellor immediately called it North Cape, the most descriptive name he could think of.

In the winter of 1664 Francesco Negri, a priest from Ravenna, Italy, arrived on foot in the polar night, becoming the very first tourist on North Cape. Millions have followed. One of them was Louis-Philippe, the later citizen king of France, who visited the cliff incognito in 1795. In 1861 Carl Vogt, a German, introduced the tradition of drinking champagne once this unique destination was reached.

North Cape recieved much publicity when King Oscar II, joint king of Sweden and Norway, paid a visit in 1873. Two years later Cook's travel agency in London arranged the first package tour. In 1893, the Norwegian coastal express steamers started calling at Hornvika Bay just below the cliff. In 1907 the king of Siam arrived.

Since the opening of the road and the modern North Cape Hall, the flow of tourists has surged to about 200,000 a year.

In small caves deep inside the mountain, North Cape's history is recreated through vivid scenes. This one shows Captain Richard Chancellor of the «Edward Bonaventure» during his hunt for the Northeast Passage in 1553. Behind him looms the landmark that he renamed North Cape.

The North Cape Hall contains restaurants, a special movie theatre, a vast gift shop, etc. A huge hall with a panorama view toward the Arctic has been blasted out of the rock.

Millions of beautiful post cards are sold. Most of them are stamped 9764 Nordkapp at the local North Cape post office.

King Oscar II leads his party on the steep climb from Hornvika Bay to North Cape in 1873.

The first tourist, Francesco Negri, arrived in 1664 (left). King Chulalongkorn of Siam had his monogram chiseled into the bedrock in 1907.

The North Cape Hall contains a special Siam pavillion, erected on the spot where King Chulalongkorn had his monogram chiseled into the rock in 1907. In 1989 the pavillion was dedicated by his grandchild, Princess Maha Chakri Sirindborn.

The bust of Louis-Philippe, placed outside a gourmet restaurant in the North Cape Hall, is a reminder of the visit by the later citizen king in 1795. He was in exile at the time, masquerading as an ordinary tourist.

A PLACE FOR EVERYBODY

North Cape is becoming increasingly popular as an international tourist destination. It started in a modest manner, with the occasional rugged individual who possessed courage, strength and the urge to discover. Then came the affluent, who could afford comfortable expeditions to this primitive, but totally unusual place. Princes and kings followed suit until ships, cars and airplanes made mass tourism possible.

Today the Germans are predominant among the nationalities who visit North Cape, followed by the Norwegians, Italians, French, British and Americans. The peak season is brief and intense: June, July and August.

There are still those who arrive in rather unusual ways: Some have walked Norway from South to North, a distance (as the crow flies) comparable to London-Gibraltar or New York-New Orleans. Another tourist jogged 4,500 kilometers from Paris to North Cape, spending 85 days on the road. A 26 year old man bicycled up from Oslo and windsurfed back again all along the coast. One sunlit midnight in 1989, a local stunt man rushed off the cliff's edge at 100 km/h (60 miles) on a motorbike. He landed by parachute in the ocean 307 meters (920 feet) below...

Some walk or bicycle to North Cape in order to create publicity for religious messages. A tougher breed of tourists come during winter, on skis, ski-scooters or by tracked vehicles.

The tourists represent a number of religious faiths. Consequently, the new chapel that was blasted out of the bedrock is consecrated as a ecumenical room for meditation, prayer and ecclesiastical ceremonies. In St. John's chapel, fittingly named after the apostle of light, one may sit down in calm to reflect upon the almost religious feelings any visitor can experience at North Cape, the top of Europe.

St. John's Chapel is the world's northernmost of its kind. It is windowless, decorated in a simple manner and has only 16 seats, yet it has become an intimate church room deep inside the mountain. Since its consecration on Midsummer Eve 1990, the chapel has been in wide use, even for weddings and christening ceremonies.

Knivskjellodden peninsula reaches out to 71° 11′ 48″, and is actually Norway's northernmost point.

However, it is far less accessible (a difficult two hour walk) than North Cape at 71° 10′ 21″ northern latitude.

Hornvika Bay holds the remnants of the world's northernmost outhouse – with proper sections for Ladies and Gentlemen.

Hornvika Bay today, with the remainders of the pier, the houses and the path spiraling toward the sky – and the North Cape plateau.

NORTHERNMOST IN EUROPE AND THE WORLD

Until the North Cape road opened in 1956, almost all tourists came by ship. They anchored in Hornvika Bay, just south-east of the cliff. The passengers were landed at a looming wooden pier, from which there was a steep, 307 meter climb up to the plateau with the famous view.

The almost 100 year old path is still visible, zig-zagging its way up a precipitous, green mountainside where reindeer graze quietly between snow patches, tumbling creeks and weather beaten boulders from ancient rock slides. On the flanks, sheer mountain walls reach toward the sky.

Most visitors made the daring ascent by themselves, but strong local boys made good money carrying the less fit on their backs.

Arriving on top of North Cape, they could all behold the vast ocean – and look across to Knivskjellodden, a tiny peninsula that juts out some 1,500 meters further to the north, making it Norway's truly northernmost point. In fact, much of what is seen in this area is the northernmost not only in Norway, but even in Europe and the world.

Looking through the characteristic Church Gate formation at Skarsvåg fishing village, you see North Cape and the Horn, a 15 meter high rock formation that in pre-Christian times served as a place of sacrifice for the Samis (Lapps).

Fredheim (Home of Peace) in Skarsvåg is the worlds northernmost religious meeting house...

No fishing village in the world is located further to the north than Skarsvåg by North Cape. Consequently, the 170 people who live here experience extremely long periods of midnight sun as well as polar darkness.

15

50 DEGREES WARMER THAN SIBERIA

On a sunny summer day the fishing village of Gjesvær 15 kms southwest of North Cape is a tranquil scene. This is the home of 230 people who subsist on the big ocean outside. The nature is wide open, with countless islands and skerries. Outermost lie Gjesværstappan with their characteristic, conical forms. These three big islands and a 500 meter zone around them have been declared a protected area due to their unique stock of sea birds and rare, subarctic flowers.

On Kjerkestappen and Storstappen, the latter rising 281 meters above sea level, there is an unusually large colony of 160,000 couples of nesting puffins.

On these and the third island, Bukkstappen, there are also more than 100,000 pairs of nesting kittiwake. In addition, there are colonies of cormorants, arctic skuas, fulmar petrels and storm petrels, gannets, seagulls, eider ducks, common guillemots and wild geese. More rare is the raven and sea eagle, sailing majestically high above the nature reserve.

On the islands you can still see tracks of tiny settlements that are several thousand years old, and notes from 1589 refer to an active church on Kjerkstappen. Gjesvær itself is described as a good harbor as early as in the saga of St. Olav (995–1030).

If, however, you should happen to see this old fishing village when the fall and winter storms are raging, the quiet appearance has vanished. In its place is a drama with thousands of towering ocean waves rolling in with the howling wind, crashing against hundreds of shoals and skerries, spraying white, salty foam all over, putting breakwaters and moorings to their test. No boat can come or go. On such days the only link with civilization is the winding road across the barren mountain behind Gjesvær. In early winter, however, the wind carries snow, and together they change the landscape. The road disappears until spring. Thus the winter storms bring total isolation to Gjesvær, where the forces of nature still have the upper hand.

In spite of these harsh facts Gjesvær, North cape and Magerøya island enjoy a relatively favorable climate. The median temperature in January is minus three degrees centigrade. That is 20 degrees above the average for coastal regions elsewhere along the same latitude, and 50 degrees warmer than areas equally far north in Siberia. Yet there is no doubt that chilly weather dominates even on Magerøya: It has frost and snow 200 days a year, plus strong wind. In summary, it explains the island's descriptive name. Magerøya means, quite literally, «The meager island».

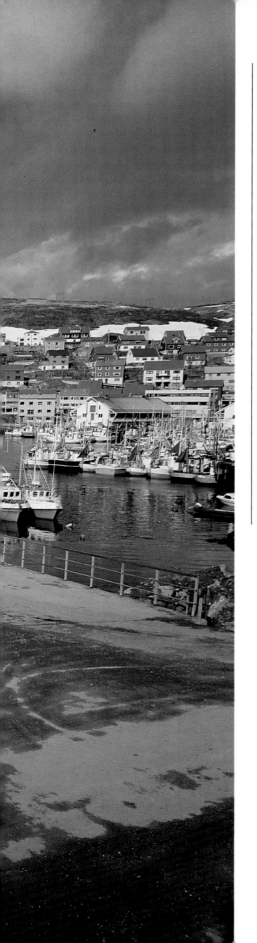

THE GATE TO NORTH CAPE

Honningsvåg (pop. 3,500) is the largest fishing village in western Finnmark. It has grown up around a natural harbor on the south-eastern part of Magerøya island. Honningsvåg was bombed by the Soviets and burned by the Germans during World War II. In 1945, only the church remained standing. Today the village is a center for fisheries, fish processing, tourism and communications, including a local airport.

Tourists have come to know Honningsvåg as «The gate to North Cape». Most visitors arrive on the Nordkapphorn, a modern ferry that carries 140 cars and 650 passengers on the 45 minute voyage from Kåfjord on the mainland. The road from Honningsvåg to North Cape is 35 kilometers, and an experience in itself. It passes by the shining white Duksfjord mountain, and all during the drive you may see groups of the 5,000 reindeer that spend the summer on Magerøya. In mid June the road is the scene of the North Cape March (70 km), which also marks the be-ginning of the week long North Cape Festival. It culminates with the traditional midnight sun dance on the pier in Honningsvåg.

This fishing village is also one of the 35 ports that the 11 combined cargo and passenger ships of the Coastal Express service (Hurtigruten) call on during their 11 day round trip Bergen-Kirkenes-Bergen. Half of this 2,500 sea mile voyage takes place north of the Arctic Circle, and leads through marvelous coastal landscapes. The ships' names, like Polarlys (Polar Light), Nordstjernen (The North Star) and Midnatsol (Midnight Sun), underscore that this route, sailed since 1893, offers unique experiences at any time of the year.

The Coastal Express, which every year carries some 300, 000 passengers, has become an indispensable link between the towns and outposts of coastal Norway. Understandably, this institution has also come to be known as «Coastal Highway No. 1». The vessels and their crews, reliable in any kind of weather, annually log a total distance equalling 36 times around the earth at the equator.

During the season, Honningsvåg harbor is packed with fishing vessels. In the summer, cruise ships line up with tourists bound for North Cape. The Coastal Express ships (above) call every day. Visible on the hillside are fences put up to prevent private houses from being crushed by avalanches...

Havøysund (pop. 1,500) is located outermost toward the Arctic Ocean between Hammerfest and North Cape. The Coastal Express calls on this tiny settlement twice a day.

Kirkenes, with its 3,800 inhabitants, is one of Finnmark's largest urban areas. It is located very close to Norway's 196 km (123 mile) long border with Russia. Kirkenes is a center for processing of iron ore.

The overturned bottom of an old boat is used as a roof – a telling memory of harder times.

Above left: One of the water-jet boats that tie this enormous county together.

DIFFICULT COMMUNICATIONS

Finnmark is Norway's northernmost, easternmost and largest county. At the same time, it has the smallest population of all 19 counties. The about 74,000 people who live here constitute about 1.8 per cent of the country's 4.2 million people, and the population density is a modest 1.6 person per square kilometer. The corresponding figure for Norway as a whole is 11 persons, compared to 25 in the United States, 233 in Great Britain and 348 in The Netherlands.

Finnmark is by nature a challenge when it comes to communications. The county has 11 airports and some of Norway's longest bridges and tunnels. The country's first undersea tunnel was blasted between Vardø and the mainland. It is almost 3,000 meters (9,000 feet) long, and takes you 88 meters (265 feet) below sea level. By 1998 a similar tunnel will tie Magerøya and North Cape to the mainland.

Boats of all kinds are used to link Finnmark's 32 towns and densely populated areas together. Such vessels are more reliable in rough weather than planes, cars and buses. In addition to the larger ships of the Coastal Express, there are local ferries and fast catamarans propelled by powerful water jets. In the summer, some of them operate tourist routes to Murmansk in Russia. These modern ferries manage well in the normally high winds and rough seas this far north.

Along the coast of Finnmark, seamen are frequently put to unusual tests due to the climate, winter darkness, treacherous low pressures and sudden fog. This is a region where intimate knowledge of the local waters – and the ability to «read» the weather correctly – are perhaps even more vital than the capability to operate radar and VHF radio.

A pretty scene from Berlevåg, eastern Finnmark, a modern fishing village that is now connected by sea, road and air to the rest of the country.

FISHING VILLAGES THAT LIVE – AND DIE

Two thirds of the population of Finnmark live in towns and heavily populated areas. Alta, Hammerfest, Vadsø, Kirkenes and Vardø are the major ones. A special feature is the large number of fishing villages located in exposed coastal regions.

There is a historical reason for this phenomenon: In earlier times, when the fishermen had to row back and forth to the fishing grounds, they settled as close to the ocean as possible. This was also the case with the Norwegians and foreigners who up until the last century lived off the rich coastal habitation of whales.

The activity at sea attracted pirates, who wrought havoc all the way eastward to the White Sea. The most notorious of them all, Jan Mendoza, passed North Cape for the final time in 1615. Then he had finally been captured and shackled in chains on a ship bound for Copenhagen, where the gallows awaited him.

In this century, a large number of people have left many of the outermost fishing villages. Big, motor powered vessels and modern technology have changed the pattern of residence dramatically. Resource and market fluctuations, along with a growing desire for greater comfort and freedom of choice, have drawn young people toward the larger population centers. As a result, many small communities now remain as deserted museums. Of particular cultural interest are the very few fishing villages that were not leveled during the war, and where the original Finnmark building style can still be seen. One of these places, Hamningberg between Båtsfjord and Vardø, is now being maintained as a tourist attraction. Kjelvik near Honningsvåg is another community that is now without permanent residents. A hurricane that in 1882 smashed even the church to pieces, contributed to the downturn. The final blow came when the whole community was scorched during World War II.

Elsewhere, many fishing villages are now thriving centers that have been tied into the all-year road and air traffic systems – and have faith in the future.

Driving north-west from Vardø, you enter a dramatic, moon-like coastal landscape. The road ends at Hamningberg, which escaped total destruction during the war. Today the population has left the fishing village, but the historically unique houses and piers remain intact. Guided tours are arranged during the summer.

23

WHITE ANGELS
OF THE OCEAN

Finnmark and Norway are facing the sea, for better and for worse. For better – because the ocean provides economic basis and possibilities for trade and communication. For worse – because the sea has always claimed lives through accidents and bad weather. In the period 1846–1855 alone, some 700 people *a year* perished in Norwegian waters.

Since 1891, the national Sea Rescue Association has guarded the coast, saving and assisting more than 350,000 persons at sea. Today this voluntary organization operates 32 effective craft and 40 shore stations, six of them in Finnmark.

These powerful boats have modern equipment and alert crews ready to cast off at any moment. The worse the weather, the more these teams are in demand. Occasionally, violent waves have smashed the wheelhouse windows on rescue boats fighting their way toward disabled ships adrift in waters turned lethal by raging forces of nature.

Improved fishing vessels and equipment, more reliable weather forecasts and the added presence of Coast Guard ships and long range Air Force helicopters have reduced the dangers of working at sea. And yet it is the compact white and red craft of the Sea Rescue Association (Redningsselskapet) that remain the very symbol of security at sea, whether they patrol the fishing grounds or stay on alert at their shore stations. With their cruising speed of 25–30 knots, they can be on the scene within a reassuringly short time.

You may be a fisherman offshore, a fisherman's wife back home or a deck hand on a tiny freighter – the certainty that a special sea rescue craft and team is never far away makes life a little easier in such exposed regions. It is not without reason that these boats of the voluntary service are affectionately referred to as *The white angels of the ocean*.

There are many dramatic and moving examples of how they have managed to pick up passengers and crews at the very last minute, and even been able to tow ships away from certain disaster. Many times the rescue teams have put their own lives on the line in order to save those of others.

Powerful rescue craft like this one are ready to go to sea when all other vessels seek harbor of refuge. These civilian vessels often cooperate with naval units and powerful, long range Air Force helicopters. For fishermen like those living in Øksfjord (right), the rescue service gives a genuine sense of security.

Hammerfest in the winter darkness that lasts for two months. Notice the special church architecture. (A photo on page 77 shows the same part of town after the razing in early 1945).

Christmas comes in the middle of the polar night, and gives a good opportunity to turn on lights everywhere. In the wake of the big fire in 1890, Hammerfest became the first Norwegian town with electrical street lights.

He enjoys life in the thriving town between the Arctic Circle and the North Pole.

THE NORTHERNMOST TOWN IN THE WORLD

Hammerfest has a polar bear in its coat of arms, and not without reason: This is the world's northernmost town, with midnight sun from May 13th until July 29th. All summer the cruise ships line up with many of the 230,000 people that visit Hammerfest during a year. The figure is impressive when one knows that this modern town on 70° 39' 48" northern latitude has only 6,900 inhabitants. Yet it is the largest of Finnmark's three towns (the others being Vardø and Vadsø).

Hammerfest developed around the best winter harbor that nature created in Finnmark. It got its town status more than 200 years ago and has always been a

Scenes like this one, with reindeer grazing peacefully in the parks, make Hammerfest different from most other cities of the world. This glimpse you will remember, whether you come from London or Liverpool, Dayton or Dallas.

junction for fisheries and coastal communications.

Fish processing is still the key industry, but a new trade is on its way: Hammerfest is the center of offshore petroleum activities in Finnmark. Supply ships and helicopters shuttle between modern shore bases and huge rigs drilling for oil and natural gas west and north of the Hammerfest region. A future field development with platforms, pipelines and onshore terminals will greatly benefit all of western Finnmark.

Hammerfest's history is dramatic: During the Napoleonic wars, the English wanted to block the grain import from Russia, and in 1809 their ships bombarded the town. In 1856 Hammerfest was razed by a hurricane, and in 1890 by fire. When the Germans withdrew in February 1945, the town was leveled to the ground. Only the graveyard chapel remained standing. Today Hammerfest is a vital, colorful center taking good care of any visitor, whether they come to do business, join the Polar Bear Society, enjoy the view from Mount Salen or see the Meridian statue, erected to commerate the first international measurement of the earth's exact size and shape.

A HISTORICAL TREASURY

West of Hammerfest, the island of Sørøya rises from the ocean like a giant breakwater. This is Finnmark's biggest island, naked, green and well known for the beauty of its scenery. The coast is cut by innumerable fjords between sheer mountain walls. Less than 2,000 people live here, and the island has only one main road. It leads from the small airport at Hasvik to Sørvær, known for its deep sea fishing festival. In July participants compete for the biggest total catch. The luckiest may return with 400 kilos (800 pounds) of fresh arctic fish, and some of the cods may weigh 20 kilos (40 pounds) each.

This rugged outpost is also known as a stone age treasury. Only a foot below the surface, scientists have unearthed thousands of rock carvings, weapons and tools that belonged to the fishermen and hunters who lived here 3,000–6,000 years ago, possibly even earlier.

Stockfish has traditionally meant business and income for the people of Finnmark.

Sørvær is one of the many idyllic spots on Sørøya. ▶

The canyon at Sautso is the most scenic part of the 170 km (100 miles) Alta/Kautokeino waterway, where anglers may catch salmon of the 20 kilo (40 pound) class. In the river, there is also a 110 meter (330 fet) high dam and a hydroelectric power plant blasted inside the mountain.

Perfect summer with calm, crystal clear water, lush pastures and luscious green deciduous forests covering the hillsides. This, indeed, is also Finnmark...

A NATURE THAT SPELLBINDS

Finnmark is the land of contrasts, whether you talk about the nature, the weather or the people who populate this outermost part of the European continent.

Everything up here is *big*. All of Denmark fits inside the county boundaries. Finnmarksvidda mountain plateau, with its 15,000 lakes of all sizes, is the largest continous wilderness area in Europe. It contains the world's best salmon rivers. One of them, the Alta river, has spent thousands of years cutting its way into the landscape. In the Sautso area it has created Europe's biggest canyon, a 15 km (9 mile) long gorge which in places is 350 meters (1,050 feet) deep.

One is constantly reminded of the dramatic forces of nature. Particularly along the coast, where arctic low pressures suddenly can unleash hurricanes that crush boats and jetties, tear roofs off houses and asphalt off roads, knock over cars, cut electric power and telephone lines and make all traffic impossible. Under such circumstances, human beings become infinitely small and fragile creatures.

The tiny settlements along the fjords are more protected, but almost disappear against the steep landscape that seems to aim at the sky. Such is Øksfjord, northwest of Alta, where Øksfjordjøkelen glacier – Finnmark's highest point – looms 1,304 meters (3,912 feet) above the small farms along the fjord. This is Finnmark's largest glacier, but far from the only cap of eternal ice in this craggy coastal area. In the summer, bluish-green melting water cascades down the mountainsides. The warm sun may even make parts of the glaciers translucent.

The Øksfjordjøkelen glacier rests with majestic calm above a handful of homes in western Finnmark. ▶

Flaming aurora borealis above the Alta fjord in western Finnmark. The light is about as bright as from a clear moon. Green is the predominant color. The energy spent in an eruption may equal 100–500 billion watts...

FASCINATING PHENOMENA

The tourists are often spellbound by the summer's midnight sun, but then they miss another and even more fascinating phenomenon, namely the northern lights or *aurora borealis*. It belongs to the darkness of fall and winter.

Northern lights are caused by enormous amounts of electrically charged particles that are hurled away from the sun. Those that hit the Earth's magnetic field are forced toward the polar regions, where they descend into the upper atmosphere. As friction builds, the particles emit energy in the form of flickering lights. It is billions of such tiny glimpses that make the bewitching flames on the northern sky.

Finnmark is located in the zone where the aurora borealis appears in its most fascinating fashion. A typical eruption has several phases: In the beginning, faint yellow-green ribbons are drawn across the sky. Then the intensity increases – a strong outbreak may illuminate the landscape much like the moon. Gradually the colors grow brighter, with red, blue and sharp green dominating the ribbons and sheets that cover much of the sky. Finally, all forces are released in a climax. At times, it appears as if space itself explodes in light and colors. Later on, sharp waves of light may tear along below the stars at speeds of 100 kilometers (60 miles) *per second*. Finally, the eruption enters a «death phase» – until the whole drama starts repeating itself.

Through the centuries, the aurora borealis has been regarded as a weather sign and source of light. It has also been a source of mystery. According to old tradition, the northern lights are linked to the realm of the dead.

No county has more intense variations between darkness and light, hot and cold, storm and calm than Finnmark. Through the ages, this has contributed to considerable superstition. As one gets to know this unusual region, one can see why.

Hot sun during the day, fierce cold during the night: Spring creates ice formations that can dwarf a solitary skier.

Loose species of rock and the weathering effect of ice, water and wind during thousands of years, have created innumerable unusual formations along the coast of Finnmark. Below is one of the more famous ones, Finnkjerka (The Finn Church) at Kjøllefjord.

The midnight sun is awesome, but not as bewitching as the northern lights.

THE REALM OF SAMI PEOPLE AND REINDEER

The picture above embodies the key elements of winter on the Finnmarksvidda mountain plateau: snow, frost, fantastic effects of light, Sami traditions – and modern technology. And space, space without limits on this rolling bedrock plain stretching high above sea level between the fjords of western Finnmark and the remote inland border with Finland.

This is the coldest area in Nor-way. Minus 51.4 degrees centigrade was measured in the Sami community of Karasjok in January 1886, and that is still the national record low. But minus 30 is not unusual, and during the four coldest months of 1966, the *median temperature* was minus 21 degrees. Then add the polar wind chill factor! In periods with severe cold, the heavy, freezing air above the mountain plateau may eventually be sucked out toward the ocean, creating ice cold storms northward through the narrow fjords.

The mountain plateau is the home of the Sami (Lapp) people and their herds of altogether 145,000 reindeer. These hardy animals live on moss and lichen that cover vast areas and are rich in proteins. The reindeer use their hoofs to scoop away the snow and get to their food.

In summer, one can see in earnest how barren this area really is. Poor, morainic soil from the last glacial age is spread out as a thin and vulnerable cover on top of the bedrock. Grass, flowers, heather and thickets of twisted mountain birches and willow cling to the ground between

Cultural contrasts: a traditional Sami tent (lavvo) with modern ski-scooters parked outside. The wide expanse, the sky and the light are, however, as they have been for thousands of years – forever unchangeable.

The mountain plateau is not as lifeless as one might think. A closer look reveals teeming, colorful biological life everywhere.

Norway's largest primeval forest is part of Øvre Pasvik national park, located between the borders with Finland and Russia.

myriads of ponds and lakes. These are truly wide open spaces.

In July, temperatures in the innermost sections of Finnmark may reach 30 degrees centigrade. That is as warm as anywhere in southern Norway.

There are several national parks in Finnmark. One of them (Stabbursdalen) protects the world's northernmost pine forest, with trees that are 500 years old. Another, in Øvre Pasvik, embraces Norway's largest primeval forest. These large pinewoods also mark the western end of the Siberian taiga.

Sandfjord in the dead of winter: Cold ocean and salty ice. Gray, weathered bedrock, sand, snow and wind – beautiful and challenging...

ARCTIC COAST AND SANDY BEACHES

If you want a close look at the county's dramatic coastal landscape, you can go east of the Tana fjord and drive the Arctic Ocean Highway from Berlevåg to Kongsfjord. You will then find yourself on the vast Varanger peninsula in eastern Finnmark, in what is truly a coastal wilderness. Off this steep coast, there are no islands or skerries to take

the brunt when winter storms send towering waves crashing against the, naked landscape.

The fishing village of Berlevåg (pop. 1,300) lies as far north as you can go on the peninsula. In earlier days, a raging ocean could tear apart the huge breakwaters sheltering the harbor. Nowadays those all-important defenses are made up of thousands of *tetrapods* – multiarmed 15–25 ton concrete slabs enmeshed with each other. It seems to do the

trick! Berlevåg has no productive land or forest, so this is one of the many outposts that are totally dependent on the sea.

The Arctic Ocean Highway runs eastward from Berlevåg through a gray landscape worn by glacial periods and extreme weather. The sandstone rock has been weathered into both exciting and grotesque formations, a mixture of geological chaos and art. In between, bluebells and buttercups grow and bloom

A bright study in blue, green, gray and white from Øksfjord in the coastal part of western Finnmark.

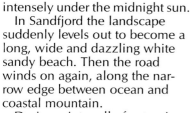

intensely under the midnight sun.

In Sandfjord the landscape suddenly levels out to become a long, wide and dazzling white sandy beach. Then the road winds on again, along the narrow edge between ocean and coastal mountain.

During winter all of nature's roughness is ironed out by snow and wind, and yet the department of highways manages to keep this unique road open practically the whole time.

In the northeast, the Finnmarksvidda mountain plateau ends at Gaissene, a string of sandstone mountains. Some of them rise to more than 1,000 meters (3,000 feet) above sea level.

A scene from the mountain plateau as it stretches out south of the key urban center of Alta.

37

A trawler on the Varanger fjord heading home with a full load of capelin after long hours far out at sea. The occurrence of capelin can vary dramatically. In rich years, it may constitute a dominant portion of the total catch in the ocean areas around Finnmark. The fish itself is only about 20 cm (8 inches) long.

Fishing can be grueling work with strong winds, darkness and icing. But it may also look like this when you head home after a long day at sea.

THE FISH INFLUENCES ALMOST EVERYTHING

Fishing has been an integral part of life in Finnmark ever since the first humans settled here some 10,000 years ago. Today, this is the main fishery county in what is still one of the world's leading fishery nations. Several hundred thousand tons of protein rich cod, pollack (coalfish), capelin and shrimp are brought ashore annually for processing and export. Here are all kinds of fishing vessels, from the smallest boats to ocean going trawlers operating north to Spitsbergen and east toward the Russian islands of Novaya Zemlya.

The ocean areas around Finnmark are unique. From the polar basin, strong currents drive cold, but very nutritious masses of water toward the south. North of Finnmark, they encounter the Gulf Stream, which right here empties its final resources of warm water from the Caribbean. In this border area polar and tropical water masses are mingled in a gigantic process. The nutri-

tious matter from the north – algae and plankton – is supplied with southern warmth and spring sunlight and starts reproducing to an enormous extent. During a single season an estimated 2.3 *billion* tons of algae is produced in the ocean outside Finnmark.

It is this abundance of nutritive substance that supports all higher life in the sea, including the fish that for thousands of years have been the basis for life along this coast. It also confirms the old saying that the further north you go, the poorer the land, but the richer the sea.

The occurrence of fish and the fishing quotas do, however, go up and down. So, as a direct consequence, does Finnmark's economy and in fact the very pulse of this county that is so dependent on nature's fluctuations. Through the centuries, the ebb and flo of the fishing industry have created wealth and tragedies, expansion and migration. This, in a way, is how it must be, because a Finnmark without fisheries is unthinkable.

39

Enormous amounts of snow have to be cut away when parts of the Finnmark road network is reopened after the winter.

Driving along the Arctic seaboard, you witness first hand how the naked coast changes in colors and shapes...

...and if you follow the inland roads, you can enjoy a more sheltered landscape with rivers full of fish and hillsides covered by birch forests that explode in green, yellow and red during the fall.

GREAT DISTANCES AND CHALLENGES

Finnmark county, larger than The Netherlands and Belgium, is also the land of great distances. The drive from Alta to Kirkenes, for example, is 520 kilometers (315 miles), or roughly like London to Land's End or Cleveland-Chicago. No wonder, then, that the people of Finnmark are used to driving very far, very often.

The main road, European Highway No. 6, is of good standard and runs all the way across the

Northeast of Alta, the E 6 runs straight as an arrow across the Sennalandet mountain plateau. The road has been partly elevated to allow the snow to blow off, but in spite of that, even this trunk road is sometimes closed when winter storms and snowfalls are particularly heavy and enduring.

county. This life nerve undulates across the main mountain plateau, meanders along deep fjords and crosses both mountains and rivers before ending by the Russian border. Other roads are not as wide, have sharper curves and less solid surface, but lower speed and more jolting is compensated by beautiful scenery. During a few hours' drive you may experience several kinds of weather, too.

In winter, polar darkness, ice and snowstorms may put cars and drivers to the test. Many roads are closed by snow drifts, and may remain shut for months. Even along main routes like the E 6, snow clearing crews may have to give in temporarily to the snowstorms – or organize the traffic in convoys escorted by huge rotating snow cutters. People who have to negotiate lonely and exposed roads when storm is threatening, bring along extra food and insulated survival suits. It may take any number of hours to locate a driver who is stuck in the night along a road that has disappeared under a heavy blanket of snow. And if the engine fails to produce warm air inside the car while the storm is raging, you may simply freeze to death. No wonder mobile telephones are popular with drivers in Finnmark.

In the fall, before the wind and snow changes the landscape, tiny bamboo poles are set along both sides of every road. The top of these markers is often the only clue the snow clearing teams have when they attempt to relocate and cut open a road that has disappeared for months.

PROUD SAMIS CARRY ON OLD TRADITIONS

The Samis (also called Lapps) populate the northernmost areas of Europe. Of these 35,000 indigenous people, some 20,000 have their homes in Norway (mainly Finnmark). 10,000 live in Sweden, 3,000 in Finland and 1,800 on the Kola peninsula in Russia. They are generally divided into four categories: *The sea Samis* are found along the fjords of North Norway, where they live by farming and fishing. *The river and lake Samis* live by the waterways in the inner parts of northern Scandinavia and have farming and fresh water fishing as their livelihood. *The forest Samis* stay in Swedish Lappland and make a living from hunting and fishing. *The mountain Samis* are found in Norway, Sweden and Finland. Their main occupation is keeping reindeer, moving their herds across long distances between the summer and winter pastures. These annual treks have taken place at least since the 16th century.

The oldest positive traces of Sami settlements in Finnmark can be dated back to about the birth of Christ. Nobody knows for certain where the Samis came from. A prominent theory points to a Siberian origin and a subsequent, gradual westward migration along the edge of the Arctic ocean. From the very beginning, the Sami culture was one of hunting and fishing, with particular emphasis on reindeer hunting and the catching of fish, seal, walrus and whale.

Today, the most distinctive group are the mountain Samis, who are the only ones who live a kind of nomadic life. In fact, their way of life is now only *half nomadic*, because the vast majority of these Samis live in permanent dwellings during most of the year. It is only during the long treks in spring and fall that their characteristic tents, the *lavvos*, are in real use any more.

Each year at Easter, the Samis get together for traditional ceremonies and celebrations. The most famous gathering is the Easter Festival at Kautokeino, in the heart of the Finnmarksvidda mountain plateau. During hectic days, the Samis arrange for trade, festivities, exhibitions, reindeer races, christenings, theatre plays, concerts with *joik* (the very special Sami way of singing) and weddings. The latter are outstanding events, with participants dressed in colorful traditional costumes in blue, red, white, yellow and black. The women wear beautiful silver jewelry. Each of the 20–30 couples may invite up to 300–500 guests to the church ceremony and ensuing procession and wedding party.

Easter always signals a new beginning: The cold, dark winter is gone, the vital light returns. The reindeer herds are on the move toward the coast and summer. It is time for festivities and weddings. Bride, bridegroom and hundreds of guests all dress in their finest traditional costumes. The women, and the bride in particular, wear many and very fine filigree brooches. The bridegroom stands out with his big, white scarf. The wedding ceremony takes place in the Protestant church.

STRONG WOMEN AND STRONG FAITH

There have always been unwritten rules about the division of labor between Sami men and women. Both have participated in fishing as well as in herding and slaughtering of reindeer. The women have processed the hides and made clothing from them. Sami women have always enjoyed an independent position, and been listened to in important matters. The rules of family relationship have been fairly complicated, and in former days there were precise guidelines regarding marriage.

Earlier generations believed in life after death, and that the souls of their forefathers took residence in certain mountains. They showed great respect for natural phenomena and worshipped the sun, wind, moon and thunder. They sacrificed to certain rocks and other nature formations in order to improve fertility and hunting skills.

In pre-Christian times the *shaman* played a powerful role as the assumed link to the realm of the spirits. He was believed to be able to cure illnesses, secure good harvests and predict the future. Through prolonged drumming and strange singing, the shaman threw himself into a state of ecstasy which would enable him to communicate with the souls and forces on the other side. The drumhead on the special magic drum was decorated with mystic symbols. They would help the shaman interpret signs and omens and decide to which power one should make the next sacrifice.

During the 18th and 19th century, the Samis became objects of rather brutal campaigns by missionairies. They resulted in wide acceptance of the Christian faith and a lasting turn toward a religious and social puritanism.

Sami women have always enjoyed an independent position, and their voices have been heard in the family councils. Today they are intent on passing the fine Sami traditions on to their children. For many years the Samis were often looked upon by others as second rate citizens. This, fortunately, is no longer the case. The Samis are now fully regarded and respected as just as Norwegian as any other citizen of the country.

Freezing cold outside, but cozy and warm inside. The climate has made the Samis experts when it comes to warm, functional clothes and tents, the latter with a big hearth for heating and cooking purposes.

A small child in a decorated cradle (komse) which provides shelter and, most importantly, ample warmth.

MASTERS AT KEEPING WARM

In former days the Samis used skis, leather boats and simple reindeer sleighs as means of transport. When hunting, they carried spears and bow and arrow as weapons. To catch fish, they used hooks, fish spears and nets. Reindeer horns and bones were used as raw material for the crude but efficient tools and weapons.

The freezing cold winters have also turned the Samis into masters at making warm, windproof clothing. The basic material has always been reindeer hides, but skins and furs of seal, fox, otter, beaver and marten have also been valuable as raw materials and trading commodities.

Today most of their ordinary clothing is made of fabric. It is cut from a common basic design, but has strong local variations with regard to colors and decorations in the way of belts, breast cloth, cap and shawl. Working clothes for summer and winter use, (in winter including footwear, furs, pants, caps and mittens), are still made from reindeer hides. Sealskin is often used for summer footwear.

The Sami tents are renowned for their ability to keep the heat from the fire. Babies stay warm and dry in their fur lined Sami cradles, and inside their winter footwear, the Samis use dried grass for insulation.

The Sami clothing made from furs and hides show great similarities with comparable clothing worn by indigenous groups in other arctic areas. Maybe they have a common origin. They are extremely effective when the temperature plummets and the wind blows across the winter landscape.

THE LONG TREK TOWARD THE COAST

Each year in April and May, the mountain Samis carry through their migration from the innermost parts of the mountain plateau to the summer pastures on the coast and big islands in western Finnmark. The gathering of the herds and the long trek may take weeks. In older days shepherd dogs were used to keep the reindeer on the move. Today ski-scooters do the job.

Every day the Samis and their flocks of hundreds, even thousands of reindeer put long stages behind them before they set up camp for the night. As the sun sinks, the shepherds build fires inside their *lavvos* – conical tents made of poles and windproof canvas – and prepare a strengthening meal. Outside, the herds rest patiently.

THE ICE COLD TRIAL OF STRENGTH

The mountain Samis constitute only about ten per cent of the total Sami population in Norway. Yet this is the best known group, due to their many animals and conspicuous way of life.

Until a few decades ago the reindeer herds had to swim across wide stretches of freezing water on the final leg of their spring trek toward the coast and the islands. It was a severe trial of strength for the animals, who were very slim after the winter and tired from trotting endlessy through the snow. Up to twenty per cent of the herds could lose the fight against currents and paralyzing temperatures in the fjords.

These days the reindeer go by boat – ferried on tank landing ships of the Royal Norwegian Navy. For four weeks in the spring, armored vehicles must wait while reindeer are shuttled across numerous fjords. Sometimes it goes on around the clock, and a single ship may take care of a total of 20, 000 animals, without losses, during «Operation Reindeer».

True, you can still see swimming reindeer herds, but only in the fall, when the animals are strong and well fed after a good summer on lush pastures. Then even the new calves are big enough to manage the strain, and the water is warmer. Hardly any animal has a problem. It is always impressive to watch as big herds cross the fjords.

It is a dramatic sight each fall when reindeer by the thousands start to swim from their summer pastures and back toward the mainland. On the beaches they start their long trek toward the vast winter quarters on the Finnmarksvidda mountain plateau.

A good looking representative of the young Samis who are to pass the unique customs and culture on to new generations.

The tank landing ships run clear up to the beach, and are perfectly suited for their seasonal role as reindeer ferries in the spring. Thereby the animals are spared long and dangerous swims through the icy water in the fjords and coastal areas.

51

Ready for a ride with reindeer from the grounds of Kautokeino Museum.

IN THE HEART OF SAMI COUNTRY

Kautokeino on Finnmarksvidda is the largest municipality in Norway. It is centrally located in the northern Scandinavian area called *Sápmi* – Sami Country (or Lappland). 85 per cent of the Kautokeino population speaks the Sami (Lappish) language, which belongs to the Finno-Ugric languages. Most of the 3,000 inhabitants, of which 37 per cent are below the age of 20, live in the villages of Kautokeino and Masi.

The municipality covers a rough mountain wilderness stretching far and wide in altitudes ranging between 400 and 700 meters (1,200–2,100 feet) above sea level. In winter, this is the coldest area in Norway. Some 100,000 reindeer belong here, and every third inhabitant is dependent upon keeping reindeer for a living. This is also the main source of trade in Karasjok, which borders on Kautokeino to the east and is the other key Sami municipality in Finnmark.

Both communities give high priority to education and culture. Kautokeino has the Sami Theatre, Sami College and Nordic Sami Institute. Karasjok is the home of the Sami Country Center, The Sami Collections and *Sametinget*, which is the parliamentary assembly of the Sami people in Norway.

A beast of prey or a friendly visitor? A Sami boy examines the tracks of an animal in the fresh snow.

The first attempts with a lasso can be a disappointing experience. But through the years, even this young man will become an accurate owner of reindeer.

This shivering cold but beautiful and imposing atmosphere, pictured in Kiby on the Varanger coast, eastern Finnmark, says a lot about the fishermen's circumstances this far north.

A busy flight of birds tells that this fisherman from Vardø has made a good catch!

A MOST IMPORTANT PROFESSION

Few waters in the world are better stocked with fish than those surrounding Norway. Vast resources have their spawning grounds just offshore Finnmark, which explains why 95 per cent of all activity along the coast is tied to the fishing trade. In Finnmark as a whole, three out of four industrial jobs are in the fishing industry. Finnmark normally contributes one fourth of the volume of the Norwegian fishing industry.

Fish are caught, brought ashore, processed and exported all year, but there are distinct seasonal peaks. In February-March, for instance, millions of capelin – a slender, silvery salmonoid about 20 centimeters (8 inches) long – move slowly toward the coast of Finnmark in order to spawn. In normal years, several hundred thousand tons of capelin are caught and processed into fishmeal and -oil. As edible fish, large quantities are being exported to Japan. Frozen hard roe of capelin is widely regarded as a delicacy.

In early spring, enormous shoals of Norwegian-Arctic cod move in from the waters farther north. They, too, are going to spawn along the coast of North Norway (a big female yields up to five million eggs). As they approach, the cod feed on the capelin already in the area. The fishing vessels catch tens of thousands of tons of protein rich cod. When processed, the filets are frozen and eventually end up on dinner tables in a number of countries on both sides of the Atlantic.

In addition to capelin and cod, the waters off Finnmark yield large quantities of pollack (coalfish), haddock, halibut, herring and shrimp, etc. Modern, ocean going vessels and high technology have made it easier to locate the resources, but at the same time the competition from foreign trawlers has become increasingly intense.

In recent years, fish breeding has become a new and fast growing business, particularly in the fjords of western Finnmark. The predominant species are salmon and trout. In other floating facilities, cod that have been caught wild offshore are being kept and fed until they have achieved the desired weight.

Fish breeding facilities become increasingly common in the fjords. The most popular and lucrative species are salmon and trout, mainly intended for export.

A good catch during fishing with Danish seine at Syltefjord. ▶

Crew members look after the closing net of a trawler. The picture was taken in the port of Honningsvåg.

Unsalted fish (mainly cod) is still hung on huge drying racks, like here at Kokelv, western Finnmark. Diminishing markets abroad have, however, made this traditional way of processing less important than before.

Shrimp production is a good example of how modern processing industry has created jobs particularly for women. This picture is from a shrimp factory in Vardø.

STILL A TOUGH JOB...

Every fisherman at sea creates jobs for five to six persons ashore. While the men dominate on the fishing grounds, the land based processing industry has provided good work opportunities for women. This is particularly the case with the modern shrimp and filet factories and the fish breeding facilities.

At the same time, more traditional ways of fish processing, like drying and salting of cod, are becoming less wide spread due to shrinking export markets.

If the onshore jobs may be monotonous, they do at least represent less danger than the activity at sea. In spite of the fact that computer technology, effective fishing gear, improved clothing and onboard living facilities make life far easier and more secure than just a few generations ago, the fisherman's work is still marked by physical hardships. In the peak season, he may work practically around the clock for a week or two before a brief and almost as busy stop in port. Then out again. Even today, boats and crews are lost at sea or harmed as the result of storms and accidents.

Modern methods make it possible to catch and deliver raw material to the processing facilities at an increasingly even rate throughout the year. This provides steady employment. On the other hand, the fishing trade is today governed by international quotas and agreements. They limit the personal initiative of the fishing skipper, but prevent excessive fishing and thereby gradual deterioration of the economic basis.

Artistic craftsmen all over Finnmark take great pride in hand-made traditional jewelry.

An example of a piece of silver jewelry made with modern technical methods, but true to the original design.

OLD CULTURE LIVES ON

Finnmark enjoys a flourishing cultural life, with theatre- and show groups and local radio stations that offer programs in the Norwegian and Sami languages. The Norwegian speaking and Sami environments have both reared a broad variety of artists of national fame. The regional human character and the many months of cold, darkness and need for indoor gathering contribute to the cultural display.

The traditions of the crafts are also strong, particularly concerning the production of home articles, jewelry and other objects made from materials like leather, silver and wood. Much of this is a continuation of Sami handicraft and designs that date back through the centuries. The only new factor is the introduction of modern technical remedies that make the production more efficient.

The local home articles are called *duodji*, which is the Sami term for items necessary for dressing, decorating, cooking, hunting and fishing. They may for instance be made of leather, and are often decorated with imprinted patterns and painted colors.

Even more prominent – and of interest to the tourists – are the artistic products of the silversmiths. Many places, but particularly in Kautokeino and Karasjok, there are silver smiths where bracelets, brooches and filigree brooches, pins and other kinds of silver jewelry are hand-made by artists. These articles are made with traditional design, but some of the craftsmen turn out additional jewelry with a highly modern style. There are also producers who make jewelry from other materials like copper, titanium, iron, horn, bone and wood.

Another specialty is knives. They, too, are based on traditional Sami design – a work of art and a highly functional tool at the same time.

Sports are part of the overall cultural picture, and Finnmark has made important contributions in this field, too. A recent example is cross country skier Vegard Ulvang of Kirkenes, who has won several Olympic gold, silver and bronze medals. Ski jumpers have done very well, too.

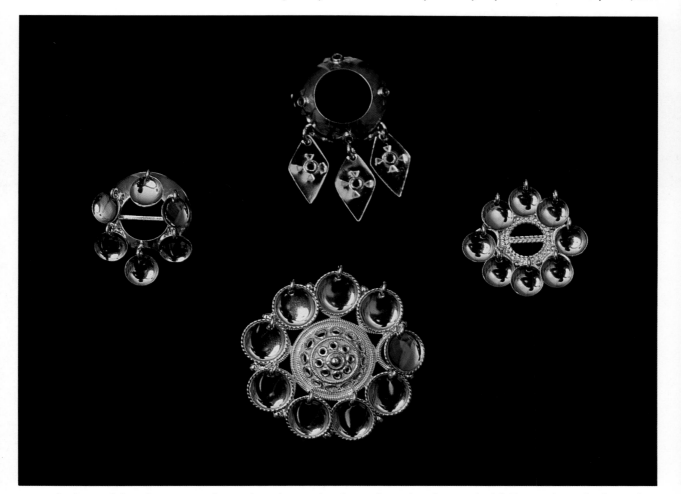

Simple, beautiful and in pure style. Such is the result when talented craftsmen faithfully combine the best of old tradition and new technique.

NEW OPPORTUNITIES ON THE HORIZON

New supports are being added to the economic life of Finnmark. Two of the most exciting and future oriented are the works of nature: The geological layers in the offshore sea bed obviously contain enormous quantities of oil and natural gas. And along the coast, on the islands, in the fjords, on the vast mountain plateau and in the national parks, Finnmark has natural attractions that already draw hundreds of thousands of tourists from all over the world. It is sufficient to mention Hammerfest, North Cape, midnight sun, northern lights, bird cliffs, reindeer and Sami traditions.

The petroleum activity is still in its initial stages. The shore base at Hammerfest and the sight of floating rigs wildcatting at sea carry promises of future expansion. Gas flames prove that discoveries of considerable reserves have already been made and are being tested. Plans have been made for vast natural gas terminals on Sørøya island, etc. Gradually, these new resources from the ocean will lubricate the economy of all of Finnmark.

The tourism sector is already humming, symbolized by the great influx of visitors arriving by cruise ship, airplane, car and bus. The season is gradually being extended beyond the summer months, and great investments have been made in hotels, tourist centers, communications and marketing. The popularity increases with the efforts to make Finnmark known as the unique area of clean and untouched nature, of wide open spaces and yet closeness to exciting phenomena. Everyone may share in the whole spectrum of outstanding experiences.

In the foreseeable future, however, the traditional industries of fisheries and mining will remain the corner stones of the economic life of Finnmark. The urban center of Kirkenes (pop. 3,800) would, for instance, be in deep trouble without the mining company of A/S Sydvaranger. With its 700 jobs, it is the largest employer in the county. The iron ore is brought in from the open works at Bjørnevatn, which has gradually been made into Europe's biggest artificial valley.

Many petroleum companies have already invested large amounts in prospective drilling offshore Finnmark. Due to the geographical and meteorological conditions in this region, the activity offers extraordinary human and technological challenges.

Royal Viking Sea is one of the many cruise ships that each year call on Hammerfest and Honningsvåg and pass North Cape en route.

Testing on Snøhvit (Snow White), a very large natural gas field north-west of Hammerfest. The ocean depth is about 330 meters (990 feet). The petroleum reserves hide in porous geological layers several thousand meters further below.

A MILD OCEAN SECURES THE HARVEST

Finnmark is located in the same northern latitude as parts of Greenland, Siberia and the northernmost coasts of Canada and Alaska. No domestic animals can be kept, no useful plants can ripen this far north on the globe – except in Finnmark.

The explanation is to be found in the surrounding ocean, where the Gulf Stream carries temperate water from the south that keeps the fjords and ports free from ice all through the winter and influences the climate far inland. In several places, the combination of protected location, fertile soil and favorable summer median temperatures make it possible, even profitable, to keep domestic animals and cultivate hardy useful plants.

This is particularly the case at the head of the fjords and in the big valleys that shelter against the winds, and where the rivers through thousands of years have carried forward and deposited soil and sand across large areas. The best protected and most fertile region is the Pasvik valley, extending south from Kirkenes between the borders with Russia and Finland. But even near Alta and to some extent in Tana, Varanger, Porsanger and Karasjok, farming communities are to be found.

The useful plants are rather simple – mainly long fodder and potatoes, but also some grain. Domestic animals are limited to cattle, sheep and chickens. There are almost no horses, and no goats or pigs. Only 0.15 per cent of the total area of Finnmark is cultivated (compared to 3 per cent for Norway as a whole). Very few people have farming as their only source of income, but a combination of farming and fishing is not uncommon.

Extra money can be made from picking berries, particularly cloudberries that thrive on the great marshes on the mountain plateau and on selected islands in the fjords. Cloudberries from Finnmark are a well known delicacy, praised for their fine taste and succulence due to the midnight sun.

Productive forests cover only two per cent of Finnmark, and forestry is almost nonexistant. All told, some 94 per cent of Finnmark is regarded as unproductive land, against an average of 74 per cent for the whole country.

Potatoes being harvested near Alta, one of the better farming regions of Finnmark.

Long fodder is among the few products that can manage this far north.

Small fields and simple crops characterize the modest farming that is possible in these sub-arctic areas. The photo shows hay drying at Nesseby near the head of the Varanger fjord.

COLORFUL AND UNIQUE FLOWERS

Mountain and beach flowers grow and bloom side by side in the coastal areas of Finnmark. This extraordinary phenomenon is caused by the special climate and other conditions of nature. In addition, this region constitutes a botanical border area between Europe and Asia. In Finnmark one will find a number of plants that are to be seen nowhere else in Norway. For that reason, too, the county is an Eldorado for botanists.

Many of the plants are small, and individually they may easily disappear between rocks and tufts of grass. If they are numerous enough, however, growing almost like blankets – which is often the case – they can dominate a landscape and add vivid red, yellow, white or green colors to an otherwise gray and barren terrain.

On these pages you will see examples of the colorful multiplicity of the flora as it always reappears following the long, dark and cold polar night.

Marsh marigold is among the first spring flowers to spring up along the creeks on the mountain plateau. Below is scentless camomile.

Rosebay willow thrives everywhere. In times of need, the root was ground and mixed with the flour.

Orchis, in northern Norway commonly called Adam and Eve, is an orchid that blooms even on North Cape.

Wood cranesbill is easy to discover with its big, light violet flowers.

Forget-me-not is named after a beautiful legend – and so, too, is the flower.

The bluebell is a hardy herb that manages well even at high altitudes.

Large parts of Finnmark are devoid of trees. In some such exposed areas, a solitary tree or two has been planted, almost in defiance. If those trees are to survive, however, they must be carefully wrapped each fall and be uncovered only when spring has definitely arrived.

The old saying that «an abundance of rowanberries means the winter will bring lots of snow» still seems to hold true.

Finnmark is renowned for its tasty cloudberries. They are rich in vitamin C and in high demand.

As nature's own contradiction this birch stands in the middle of the treeless Finnmarksvidda mountain plateau. It carries every sign of a struggle against wind and weather.

Dandelion is a weed, even in Finnmark. However, in large quantities, it becomes decorative.

The Finnmark bog myrtle has a strong fragrance. Stemming from Asia, it can grow quite high.

Black bearberries make the mountains turn red in the fall. The hardy species has grown here since the ice age.

TEEMING BIRD CLIFFS AND WILD ANIMALS

The precipitous bird cliffs of northern Norway are widely known, and not without reason: On these craggy formations rising straight out of the ocean, millions of birds are nesting. Gannet, guillemot, puffin, cormorant, kittiwake, razorbill, fulmar, arctic skua, etc. build their nests side by side in small depressions, crevices, on tiny shelves and underneath rocks. In the teeming colonies the female birds brood while the air is filled with males flying back and forth between the nest and the food resources in the sea.

Most of the bird cliffs are inaccessible to human beings, and those who try to climb them risk being viciously attacked. One exception is the bird reserve on the relatively flat Store Ekkerøy island east of Vadsø, where you can drive to the general area and follow marked trails through the colonies.

The bird cliffs are all facing open stretches of ocean where polar currents mingle with temperate water, creating superb conditions for massive reproduction of plankton and algae. This attracts small fish who in turn are snatched away and end up in the wide open beaks of newly hatched birds back on the cliff.

It is quite fascinating to be in a boat and study these packed and always vibrating bird societies at close range. One wonders how it is possible for the males to fly in from the ocean, loaded with fish, and always land at precisely the right one among, say, 65,000 similar nests...

The numbers are totally different when it comes to the larger animal species on the mainland. The Pasvik valley and the inner parts of the Finnmarksvidda mountain wilderness is the home turf of a large portion of Norway's estimated 200 brown bears. They hibernate from October to April-May. During the summer they roam about vast areas, often crossing into Finland and Russia. Being the largest and strongest beasts of prey in Norway, they normally eat just roots and berries, but may also kill both moose (elk) and sheep. The brown bear is totally protected in Norway. Permission to hunt is granted only if it has been documented that an individual bear has become a clear danger to domestic animals and humans. The Samis used to regard the brown bear as a half human, half divine creature.

Flapping wings fill the air by the bird cliff. The surface is almost covered by nests, down, eggs and nesting females. The noise can be overwhelming.

This little fellow proves that the brown bear is surviving in Norway. Fully grown he will weigh about 250 kilos (500 pounds).

The horned grebe nests in the sheltered marshlands of Pasvik. Elsewhere it is seen only sporadically.

The greenblack great cormorants belong to the pelican birds. They live by fish, and are believed capable of diving 90 meters (270 feet) below the surface.

▶

The king eider is an arctic species. It nests on Spitsbergen, but when the archipelago is ice bound in November, it is forced southward to Finnmark. The male is characterized by the big knoll on its forehead.

◀*The golden eagle reigns in the inner areas of Finnmark. It lives by hare, gallinaceous birds and carcasses of reindeer and sheep. On the coast one finds the gray sea eagle, Norway's biggest bird of prey.*

The boreal owl nests in the areas along the Finnish border. It hunts mice and lemmings during the night.

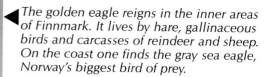

The northern (red-necked) phalarope is common. The male manages both brooding and child care.

The puffin – also called the parrot of the sea – may ◀*nest in colonies comprising 20,000–200,000 couples.*

Following the last ice age, the reindeer was one of the first mammals to enter Norway. It always appears in groups, and can endure harsh climate. These reindeer are enjoying the sea on Sandfjord beach, eastern Finnmark.

In former days the wolf was quite common, and played a dubious role in fairy tales and legends. Today there are just a few roaming animals left in all of Norway.

A common seal rests at the mouth of Tana river. This species can become 180 cm (70 inches) long, swim 65 km/h (40 m/h) and stay submerged for up to half an hour.

The lynx is Norway's only member of the wild cat family. A lone hunter who operates at night.

The brownish lemming is a plump and ill-tempered little rodent living in the mountains. Some years the stock grows enormously, triggering mass migrations toward lower areas and the sea.

The otter lives along creeks, rivers and ocean beaches. A good swimmer and a night animal. Loves fish.

The red fox is a cunning animal of prey and quite common in large parts of Finnmark. It eats carcasses, small rodents, birds, fish and berries. Here are two curious cubs outside their lair.

73

This and other Sami places of sacrifice have been found at the head of the Varanger fjord. In addition, remainders of almost 200 primitive dwellings have been uncovered in the same area.

AN IMPORTANT PART OF THE WORLD HERITAGE

People have lived along the coast and fjords of Finnmark since thousands of years before the birth of Christ. The remainders of many primitive settlements and tools dating back to the older stone age have been uncovered. Particularly interesting discoveries have been made at Mount Komsa near Alta. *The Komsa culture* is used as a common name for all these settlements, which are among the oldest in the whole country.

Exciting finds of more recent dates have also been made. In 1973 the first of several major fields of rock carvings was detected at Alta – purely by accident. These fields comprise a total of about 5,000 rock carvings that are 2,500–6,500 years old. These represent reindeer, moose (elk), bears, boats, fishing gear, weapons, people, etc. Some carvings show hunting scenes, others men and gear aboard boats. Several figures appear to have religious significance.

In 1985 the main rock carving field at Hjemmeluft in Alta was entered on UNESCO's distinguished inventory of the cultural treasures of the world that are most worthy of preservation, The World Heritage List. The primitive stone age figures on the slopes of naked rock near Alta are the only prehistoric traces that have been included from the entire Nordic area.

Quite naturally, it was the coast, with its relatively mild climate and good potential for communication, hunting and fishing that attracted the first humans who approached this region following the last ice age. Nobody knows for sure from where they came. Some maintain it could have been from the southeast, others believe they moved north along the coast of Norway. Maybe the unknown settlers came from both directions, but not at the same time during the many thousands of years before the dawn of the Christian era.

There is, incidentally, little reason to believe that there is any link between the Komsa and the Sami cultures. The Samis arrived much later, probably after a prolonged westward trek from Asia or Siberia along the coast of the Arctic Ocean. They reached the milder shores of Finnmark long after the Komsa people had established the settlements that have been rediscovered in our own time.

Already in the stone age the people of Finnmark knew how to handle boats. But what kind of equipment does the man in the rear hold in his hands?

There is a lot of drama in this hunting scene involving reindeer and man. It was scratched into the rock surface by an unknown artist thousands of years ago. The UN organization for culture, UNESCO, counts the Alta carvings among the treasures most worthy of preservation.

OCCUPATION AND SCORCHED EARTH POLICY

When Hitler's forces attacked Norway on April 9th 1940, the northernmost landings took place at Narvik. The fighting there lasted for two months, and only later on did German troops enter Finnmark. The buildup there reached a climax when Hitler attacked the Soviet Union in June 1941. German armies in Finnmark pushed eastward through northern Finland and started what was to become a bitter trench warfare against the Red Army on the *Arctic Front* in the forbidding wilderness between Kirkenes and Murmansk.

Toward the end of 1941, Hitler began fearing an Allied invasion of North Norway. At the same time, Allied convoys carrying thousands of tons of war supplies started leaving North America on the dangerous run around Finnmark to the Soviet ports of Murmansk and Archangel. In early 1942, *der Führer* began ordering massive transfers of troops, aircraft and the heaviest units of the German navy to bolster his *Fortress Norway*, particularly in the north. Huge coastal defenses and naval bases were built, not least in Finnmark. As a result, allied convoys suffered dramatic losses.

The British Secret Intelligence Service (SIS) trained Norwegians as agents and landed them to report on the German fleet. The Russians did much the same. Soviet submarines and aircraft hammered German ships and installations. Kirkenes was bombed more frequently than any other urban area in Europe!

From the spring of 1943 many of Hitler's largest warships used the fjords near Alta as their bases. In September British midget submarines managed to penetrate the steel nets protecting the *Tirpitz* – sister ship of the *Bismarck* – and severely damaged the 42,000 ton battleship. Then followed a series of bombing attacks on her from aircraft carriers off Finnmark and bases in the Soviet Union. 60–70 planes performed day or night attacks, well aided by local secret agents. Finally Hitler's top ship was towed south to Tromsø – and sunk there by the RAF Bomber Command.

During Christmas 1943, Norwegian SIS agents in Alta radioed that the battle cruiser *Scharnhorst* left its protected base and headed north. In a full gale and the polar darkness of the Arctic Ocean, she was sunk by a joint British-Norwegian naval force in *The Battle of North Cape*.

In late 1944, the Germans withdrew from the Arctic front and northern Finland. They were pursued by Soviets troops and aircraft, which also bombed many Norwegian towns and villages occupied by the Germans. Hitler decided that Finnmark had to be evacuated by force and destroyed to slow down the Soviet advance. The population of about 50,000 was to be shipped south, but almost half of them managed to seek refuge on the islands, in the mountains, inside caves or mines – where some died and others were born.

11,000 homes, 116 schools, 27 churches and 21 hospitals were singed, all domestic animals slaughtered, all boats wrecked, bridges and piers systematically blown apart. With few exceptions, *The Scorched Earth Policy* was executed everywhere before the Red Army reached the rubble heaps of Kirkenes and continued westward, while the Germans put up a new line of defense in Troms county. An unusually mild winter prevented a catastrophe among those civilians who had defied Hitler's orders and stayed behind in the seared wilderness of Finnmark – totally without housing, livelihood, clothing, medicine, food and heat.

Gradually, they were aided by the Russians (who later withdrew completely), and by free Norwegian and British military forces, before a painful rebuilding process could begin. There are still innumerable traces of World War II in every part of Finnmark.

Warships stand by as families are forced away from their homes in the fall of 1944.

Thousands defied Hitler by seeking refuge in the mountains, in caves and even mines.

Hammerfest at war's end in 1945. The photo on page 26 shows the same scene 45 years later.

Mother and child have sought refuge underneath an upturned boat. Others lived in caves.

No group suffered more during the war and occupation 1940–1945 than the people of the totally devastated county of Finnmark.

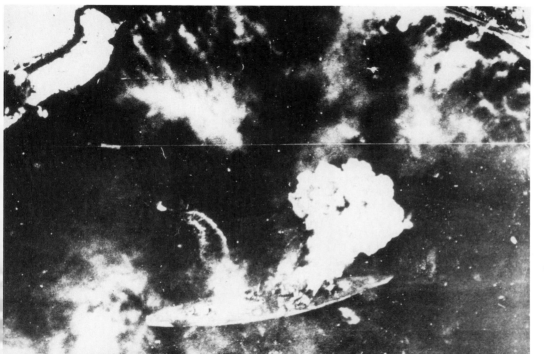

The battleship Tirpitz under attack by British bombers in Kåfjord near Alta.

PICK AND CHOOSE YOUR WINTER ADVENTURE

Finnmark is the «wild» part of Norway. Everywhere in the county varied outdoor experiences are available, all year.

When snow covers the mountain plateau, you can learn how to handle huskies, then take off with your own team, or go along as passenger on a dog sleigh. On a longer trip, you may experience ice fishing and visit Samis in their winter quarters. In some places you may go into a *lavvo* and sit down on a reindeer skin

while meat and marrow bones are prepared in a big kettle over the fire. You may even try the famous Sami wedding dish of *bidos*. You may stay overnight in a tent or show cave.

It is quite possible to rent your own reindeer and sleigh. At Easter, you may enter the tourist division and participate in the popular reindeer races at Kautokeino. You are guaranteed a lot of fun!

Ski-scooters and other snow vehicles provide the tourists with a wide range of action, whether they want to visit North Cape during winter, ice fish or ski in

the wilderness. Enthusiasts from all of Europe participate in the annual 600 km (360 miles) ski-scooter safari through the northern parts of Finland, Sweden and Norway. Others participate in more local, but no less breakneck ski-scooter rallies.

March is the time for the annual *Finnmarksløpet*, which is Europe's toughest dog team race. The participating men and women and their 6–18 dogs cross 1,000 kilometers (600 miles) of mountains, forests, ice covered lakes and rivers. The course follows the old mail routes across the mountain plateau. The

Every Easter Eve Samis of both sexes and all ages participate in reindeer racing at Kautokeino. Tourists may participate in their own class.

Skills and ability for quick reaction are put to the test in the many ski-scooter competitions with tough going in deep snow and biting cold.

Tourists have a number of different ways to taste life in the wilderness. One of them is to rent your own dog team or go along as passengers.

race starts and ends at Alta, and the best teams use five days and nights on the round trip. Those who complete the race will long remember the icy winds, the fabulous light and scenery – and the many strains of this extraordinary endurance test.

One may also seek milder challenges in the way of ski trips between cozy tourist huts – you may even let yourself be towed by a reindeer, a dog team or a ski-scooter. The best time for all of this is in the «spring-winter» from March to May, with glittering sunshine, long days and still good skiing.

ACTIVE SUMMER

Close contact with nature is a great and obvious part of life for everyone in Finnmark county. Many get aquainted with its magnificent nature even before they can walk, just like the little fellow below...

The alternatives stand in a queue, particularly in summer: windsurfing, skin-diving, boat-life and all kinds of fishing on the coast and in the fjords. Riverboat- and photo safari, rafting, canoeing, gold washing and fishing along the salmon rivers. Hang-gliding and climbing rugged mountains. Hunting, fishing, hiking and trips into the wilderness with horses or pack dogs. In good summers, you may even go for a swim in this country bordering on the Arctic Ocean.

All this activity is available without waiting in line and in vast, untouched areas with clean water, clear air and a unique, natural calm that soon fills the people who come here. Of course, nothing is perfect all the time: On the coast, polar fog may suddenly roll in and cover the summer sun and view for a while. And on the mountain plateau, the mosquitos are intensely active in early summer. That area is, however, at its best from late July until mid September. Then it is no longer the mosquitos, but the many and fascinating colors that dominate the landscape.

There is nothing like starting young...

The mountains are meant to be used.

80

In Mattisdalen valley near Alta you may rent horses and head into the fabulous wilderness waiting just beyond.

Beach life at Grense-Jakobselv in Varanger, where the border river between Norway and Russia meets the Arctic Ocean.

Such is the salmon you can get in the Alta river. This one was caught with a net.

AN ANGLER'S PARADISE

Finnmark is any angler's wonderland. Whether you prefer the ocean, the coast, the fjords, rivers or lakes – you can be sure of excitement and a good catch.

Salmon and trout are the most distinguished species. In several thousand kilometers of river you can catch these «aristocrats» either from the bank or a boat – once the fishing permit is in order. The world record for salmon caught by rod was set in Tana river. The fish weighed 36 kg. (72 lb).

Finnmark has 60 000 lakes and ponds, most of them stocked with trout, char, grayling and pike.

If you prefer salt water, it is easy to go out with a rented boat and catch big cod or nasty looking catfish by North Cape or try your luck with the pollack (coalfish) near Hammerfest. You may also participate in one of several deep sea fishing festivals. If, on the other hand, you prefer being by yourself, your chances are excellent: Finnmark has plenty of islands and exciting coastline to choose from. You are assured fine experiences and lots of fish.

Those who fish out on the ocean quite often get cod, haddock and pollack of rather grown-up sizes. Large quantities of catfish (wolf fish) are also caught. In spite of a rather frightening appearance, it is a very tasty edible fish.

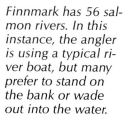

Finnmark has 56 salmon rivers. In this instance, the angler is using a typical river boat, but many prefer to stand on the bank or wade out into the water.

HERE YOU MAY PAN YOUR OWN GOLD

For somebody arriving from far lower latitudes, it is a pleasant surprise to see the many marinas that have popped up in different parts of Finnmark. They can be as full of boats and teeming with life as any yacht harbor on the sunny coast of South Norway. Likewise, it is a pleasure to watch Norway's oldest and largest sailship, the *Staatsraad Lemkuhl*, round North Cape on a tourist trip with all sails set. But there is more to be excited by:

In 1866, gold nuggets were discovered in the river sand at Karasjok, and by the turn of the century, commercial extraction was going on. Today, gold panning – tourist style – is offered both here and by Anarjohka River. During *Karasjok Open* in July, participants pan for gold in the river at Karasjok on Saturday, then sort carefully through the sand and soil at Helligskogen all day Sunday. The object of the competition is to find the most nuggets and win a valuable traveling trophy.

Cruise ships are impressive and comfortable, but it is even more exhilarating to view North Cape from the deck of a three- masted bark...

The small-boat marina in Alta. Except for the license plates, this photo could just as well have been taken in one of the typical «summer towns» on the south coast of Norway.

Gold panning normally yields high tension, low profits and cold fingers. Some still hope, however, to discover the main vein that runs near Karasjok – according to legend.

Summer in the polar land. Night with golden light, mild air and fragrances of salt ocean, fresh kelp and coffee just made on a driftwood fire. Silence in the nature, calm in the soul. Can you ask for anything more?

Gunfire can still be heard from Vardøhus fortress in Vardø, but it is only to mark the end of the polar night.

Radar stations in Finnmark monitor the ocean areas and airspace around North Norway and the vast military bases on the Kola peninsula in neighboring Russia.

THE LAND BETWEEN EAST AND WEST

Finnmark forms the spearhead of NATO's northern flank. Right here, in midnight sun and arctic darkness, military aircraft from east and west patrol the same airspace above the ocean. On the surface and in the deep, cruisers, carriers and nuclear submarines perform their missions. The Kola peninsula just east of the Norwegian-Russian border still holds the world's largest military base complex. This is where the vast Northern fleet has its ice free ports, nuclear arsenals and huge facilities inside mountains. There are more than 20 airfields on Kola and several specialized attack divisions.

On the Norwegian side, coast guard vessels, submarines, surveillance aircraft and radar stations at Honningsvåg, Kautokeino, Vardø and North Cape act as NATO's eyes and ears toward the north and east. They are on constant alert, even though the tension in this strategic field of intersection has become far lower than during the cold war. In those days, Soviet forces could make threatening moves toward Norway across land and sea or through the air. Since the Soviet Union dissolved itself and Russia

in 1992 became Norway's new neighbor in the northeast, the political climate has grown milder: the common and still guarded border has gradually been opened to trade and tourism. Simultaneously, the military readiness on both side has become less visible.

Norwegian patrol at boundary marker 184. The Russian markers along the 196 km common border are painted in green and red.

Still the geography remains unchanged, with Finnmark prominently positioned in a forward border area of great international military, political and economic importance. So far *Vardøhus* – the octogonal, star shaped entrenchment in the world's northernmost fortified town – remains the only defense installation that has obtained museum status. The initial version was built in the 14th century, to shield against the threat from the east. The present fortress was constructed in 1734–38. One of its many cannons is still being fired, but only once a year: it is as a salute of joy around January 20th, when the entire sun disc is once again visible above the horizon following two months of polar night. On that day schools are out, and every student may make three wishes...

Beside the commandant's house at Vardøhus a solitary, planted rowan clings defiantly to the ground – the only tree in this old, historical town located further to the north than Murmansk and further east than St. Petersburg. Each fall, the tree is wrapped very carefully, and for a good reason: Vardø is the only town in Norway that lies inside not only the polar, but even the *arctic* climate zone.

Meeting at high level: an F-16 fighter of the Norwegian Air Force intercepts a Russian «Backfire» jetbomber
off the Norwegian coast. In some years, Norwegian
pilots have been scrambled on more than four hundred such «hot» missions. Fighters on Quick Reaction
Alert are airborne in a few minutes.

Fast missile-torpedo boats with great striking power
constitute an important part of the anti-invasion defenses of North Norway. Armed with guns, advanced missi-
les and torpedoes these vessels are suited for maritime
guerilla between islands and in the fjords. Their crews
know the area and conditions of nature by heart.

IN HISTORICAL LIGHT

On Vadsøya island, which is part of the town of Vadsø on the north shore of the Varanger fjord, a towering metal construction stands reaching aimlessly toward the sky.

In reality, this is a mooring mast for airships. Today, it serves in part as a monument commemorating the great Norwegian explorer Roald Amundsen and his last major polar expedition. It took place in 1926, when he went along with the airship *Norge* (Norway) on its flight across the North Pole. The expedition was headed by Amundsen, the Italian airship designer Umberto Nobile and the American pilot and polar explorer Lincoln Ellsworth. The crew were Norwegians.

The airship was flown from Italy via Oslo and Leningrad to Vadsø, where the 106 meter (318 feet) gas filled craft hung tied to the mooring mast during its last preparatory stop on the mainland. Then the *Norge* continued to Ny-Ålesund on the arctic archipelago of Spitsbergen. This tiny settlement became the departure point of the first trans polar flight in history. The North Pole was passed on May 12th, and after three days of flying, the airship landed at Teller, Alaska.

In 1928 Nobile used the mast at Vadsø for his own airship, the *Italia* (Italy), which soon after went down in the Arctic. Nobile survived, but Amundsen lost his life while trying to rescue his friend by airplane.

A historical light is shining even on Nesseby church (opposite page), which is surrounded by the Varanger fjord on three sides. The church stands on an old Sami sacrificial site, and does in a way commemorate the work of Thomas von Westen. Nicknamed «The apostle of the Samis», he was an uncompromising Norwegian priest who early in the 18th century used harsh methods to convert the Samis to Christianity.

The airship mast has become a landmark in Vadsø (pop. 6,000), which is Finnmark's county capital and second largest town. Vadsø has many memories of the large Finnish immigration and the enduring pomor trade with the Russians. In 1940–44 the town was bombed repeatedly by the Soviets, and totally demolished when the Germans withdrew in October 1944.

FROM WITCHCRAFT TO MODERN CHURCH

Traditionally, there has been quite a lot of paganism and superstition in Finnmark. There have been witch hunts, too, climaxing in the 17th century: in the Vardø area alone, 80 women were found guilty of witchcraft and sentenced to death by fire. Mount Domen, south of the town, was regarded as the Brocken of the North. The witches assembled here to have rendevouz with the Devil himself, who lived in a cave...

The religious activity in Finnmark today is strong and multifarious. For example, there is a Catholic church in Hammerfest, an ecumenical chapel at North Cape and the St. George's Chapel – the only Greek-Orthodox house of worship in Norway – at Neiden in the greater Kirkenes area. This is the home of the remaining 300–400 *skolte* Samis (East Samis) in Norway. They used to constitute the entire population of this region. In the Nordic area, most skolte Samis now live on the Kola peninsula in Russia, but they are also represented in northern Finland. All have strong ties to the Orthodox church. St. George's Chapel at Neiden, built in the 1500s, is probably the oldest building in Finnmark.

There are many other denominations and religious communities in Finnmark. One of them is named after its founder, Lars Levi Læstadius (1800–1861). His movement is well entrenched in parts of the county, and is known for its rather puritanical look on life.

The Greek-Orthodox chapel (right) lies where the Neiden river meets the Neiden fjord. The border with Finland runs just ten kilometers (six miles) further south. The picture above shows an annual ceremony in the river.

The Norwegian (Lutheran) state church, the Methodist church, the Roman Catholic, Russian Orthodox and Anglican church were represented when St. John's Chapel at North Cape was consecrated in June 1990. (See also page 13).

Many roads lead to church. Here a wedding party en route on the Tana river.

North Cape has been drawn and painted for centuries. This is a water-color by A. F. Skjøldebrand, dated 1799.

A WORLD OF DRAMA AND LEGEND

At all times, audacious seafarers have sailed around North Cape. It is the hope of making new discoveries and fortunes that have made them challenge the forces of nature in this utterly exposed region. Many found an early grave just here – pulled under at sea or smashed against land by violent storms. Those who perished are all forgotten, but among those who did return, some are still alive in memory.

One of them is Ottar, a local chief and explorer in the ninth century. He lived «northernmost of all Norwegians» and undertook a voyage around the northern tip of Norway. He continued east to the White Sea and returned with hides and furs. Ottar's detailed report, requested by King Alfred the Great of England, can still be studied at The British Museum in London.

The Vikings, who are otherwise best known for their long expeditions to the Mediterranean, the Black Sea and North

America, passed North Cape in their open boats as early as A.D. 800–900. They, too, continued east around the Kola peninsula and to the area where the city of Archangel is now located. Not all expeditions were peaceful. St. Olav's saga tells about Karle from Langøy and Tore Hund from Bjarkøy who sailed with two ships and a hundred men to the White Sea to trade goods. On their return trip they plundered a Russian sanctuary of its treasures – and started quarreling about how to share the loot. At

At Gjesvær by North Cape, where there is still a fishing village, the Vikings Tore Hund and Karle quarreled about the treasures thay had stolen further east. Tore killed Karle with a sword, as seen here in the old saga.

Many stories were told of the great fisheries in the high latitudes. This drawing from 1555 adds to the image: the halibut and some of the cods are almost as large as the fishing vessels that got them...

Darkness, towering waves and northern lights all added to frightening legends about monsters that swallowed men and boats. The stories lived on, because vessels and crew often did disappear mysteriously. Drawing from 1555.

Gjesvær (page 16–17) just west of North Cape, the saga says, they went ashore to settle the disagreement. It ended quickly when Tore Hund drove his spear *Selsbane* all the way through Karle and killed him on the spot.

From the Middle Ages, there are numerous legends about the Russian *tsjudes* who plundered and killed at will on their wild expeditions along the coast of Finnmark. They were «bloodthirsty as wolves», but the Norwegians learned how to ambush them. Reddish stone walls accor-

ding to old belief, taken eternal color from the blood of the tsjudes...

Legends particularly tell about two large brothers at Tunes near North Cape who fought back 50 tsjudes. The brothers used boat masts as weapons, killing 22 Russians before the others fled. On Christmas Eve some years later the tsjudes returned, killed the two and stole a halibut of solid silver. It had been forged by the Tunes brothers and given to the church as thanksgiving because The Lord had heard their

prayers while at sea during furious weather.

Just as frightening as the tsjudes were the conceptions of enormous sea snakes and other monsters that could emerge from the ocean and swallow both ships and crew. Dating ages back is the frightful *draugen*, the ghost of a drowned person who comes sailing in half a boat when the sea is in uproar and men are in distress. When *draugen* turns his skull and stares at you with his empty eye sockets, you know that death is very near...

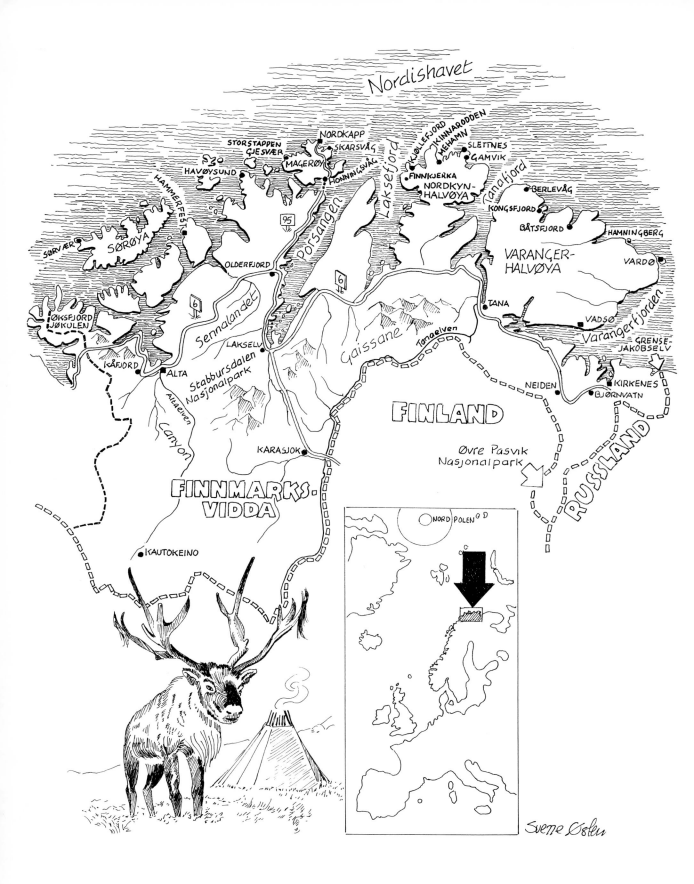

PHOTO CREDITS

Aune: 86 (1)

Caprino, Ivo: 10, 11 (3,4)

Emfem/Dahlslett: 40 (3), 41, 60, 64 (1), 80 (2)

Emfem/Reisnes: 26 (3), 28/29, 35 (1), 80 (1)

Forsvaret, Fotosentralen: 86 (2,3), 87

Frislid, Ragnar: 72 (2), 73 (1,2)

Gullhav, Henning: 41 (1), 67 (2), 90

Hjemmefrontmuseet: 76 (2), 77

Hydro Media: 61 (2)

Nationalmuseum, Stockholm: 92

Nicolaisen, André: 4

PANFILM/Raymond Mortensen: 6/7, 14 (2), 16/17, 18, 56 (1,2), 58 (2), 61 (1), 62 (2), 65 (1,2,4), 67 (3), 78, 79 (1), 82, 85

Rapp, Ole M.: 25, 26 (1), 31, 32, 44, 45, 50, 53 (2), 64 (3), 65 (2), 66 (1,3,4), 67 (2), 83, 84

Redningsselskapet: 24

Riksarkivet: 76 (1)

Roxrud Billedarkiv: 2/3, 20 (3), 27, 28 (1), 59, 66 (2), 81 (1), 30 (1)

Røe Foto A/S: 5, 8 (3), 9, 12, 13, 20 (1), 34, 43, 48/49, 53 (1), 58 (1), 62 (1), 81 (2), 11 (2)

Samfoto: 22 (1) (Bård Løken), 22 (2) (Pål Hermansen), 35 (1) (Jan Arve Dale), 36 (Bård Løken), 37 (1,2,3) (Ragnar Frislid), 40 (2) (Bård Løken), 46 (1) (Pål Hermansen), 46 (2) (Hans Hvide Bang), 47 (Hans Hvide Bang), 51 (1) (Aslak Aarhus), 51 (2) (Mimsy Møller), 63 (Ragnar Frislid), 64 (2) (Pål Hermansen), 68/69 (Pål Hermansen), 69 (2) (Hans Hvide Bang), 70 (1,2) (Bård Løken), 71 (2,4) (Bård Løken), 72 (3) (Jostein Grastveit), 73 (4,3) (Jan Rabben), 74 (2) (Tore Wuttudal), 75 (Steinar Myhr), 89 (Bård Løken)

Scribe A/S: 8 (1,2), 11 (1), 14 (1,3), 15, 91 (1)

Sveen, Arvid: 20 (2), 21, 23, 26 (2), 30 (2), 33 (1,2), 38, 39, 42, 52, 54 (1), 54 (2), 55, 56 (3), 57, 72 (1), 74 (1), 88, 91 (2)

TO-FOTO A/S: 19, 33 (3), 70 (3), 71 (1,3)

Typesetting and reproduction: Grafisk Sats & Repro a.s, Oslo
Printed by Centraltrykkeriet Grafisk Service AS, Norway
Binding: Norbok a.s
Translated and edited by: Scribe A.S
Layout: Sverre Østen
Cover Photos: Aune
Cover vignettes: Samfoto (Bård Løken), Arvid Sveen, Ole M. Rapp
Photo Credits: Page 95

© Scribe A.S/Ernst G. Mortensens Forlag A.S, 1992

ISBN 82-527-1204-5

ERNST G. MORTENSENS FORLAG A.S